Bɾ

Science Experiments

COLOR

by
John Farndon

BENCHMARK BOOKS

MARSHALL CAVENDISH

NEW YORK

Marshall Cavendish Corporation

99 White Plains Road

Tarrytown, New York 10591

© Marshall Cavendish Corporation, 2001

Created by Brown Partworks Ltd

Library of Congress Cataloging-in-Publication Data

Farndon, John

    Color / by John Farndon
    p. cm. — (Science experiments)
    Includes index.
    Summary: A collection of experiments that explore the nature of
color and how it is created and perceived.
    ISBN 0-7614-1092-9 (lib. bdg.)
    1. Color—Experiments—Juvenile literature. [1. Color—Experiments.
2. Experiments.] I. Title.

QC495.5 F47 2000   99-086994
535.6'078—dc21

Printed in China

PHOTOGRAPHIC CREDITS

t – top; b – bottom; c – center; l – left; r – right

AKG: p4, (tr)
Corbis: p12, 13 (b)
Dolland and Aitchison: p23 (t)
The Image Bank: p22, Craig van der Lende (b); p26, 27
Funk, Mitchell (b)
Rex: p20, (b)
SPL: p27, Hank Morgan (r)
Martin Norris: p21
Telegraph Colour Library: title page, B. Losh (c); p16, B. Losh (bl)
Tony Stone: p4, Jon Nicholson (b); p8, Lester Lefkowitz (b)

Step-by-step photography throughout: Martin Norris

Front cover: Martin Norris

Contents

WHAT IS COLOR?

Did you know?

Rainbows curve into perfectly arced "bows" because the raindrops that reflect them are round. From the ground, you only see a half circle. But if you go up in an airplane and look down on clouds, you may be able to see a rainbow forming a complete circle on the tops of the clouds.

The world is a very colorful place, but when we see colors what are we actually seeing? Some colors are vibrant: bright blue skies, or shocking pink Lycra clothes. Others are more subdued: the browns of a plowed field, or the grays of a freeway. All these colors are actually light.

Light travels in vibrations, or waves. The waves are incredibly tiny, varying from just 400 to 700 nanometers (nm) in length. A nanometer is a billionth of a meter—so short that you could fit a million across a pinhead.

All the different colors you see are tiny waves like this with slightly different lengths. Red is the longest (about 700 nm); violet is the shortest (about 400 nm). All the other colors have wavelengths in between.

When you see the violet light given out by a fly-deterrent light in a grocery store, you are seeing short waves of light. When you see a red traffic light, the waves making up the light are nearly twice as long. A green traffic light sends out waves of light that are midway between these two extremes.

The vibrant colors of a windsurfer's sail, board, and safety clothes have a practical use: they contrast strongly with the color of the sea, so that in an emergency he will be easy to spot.

In focus

RAINBOWS
Sunlight looks completely colorless, but it is actually a mixture of every single color, with waves of different lengths jumbled together. This light, a mixture of every color, is called white light. It comes from the Sun, from flashlights, and from fluorescent lights. Scientists know that white light contains every color because they can split it up into the colors of the rainbow.

Rainbows are the reflection of the Sun in raindrops. This is why they appear in showers of rain, and you can only see them when you stand with your back to the Sun. You see rainbows because of the way the raindrops bend and reflect white sunlight.

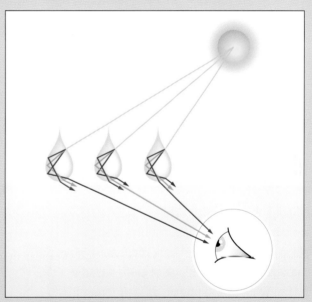

When rays of white sunlight shine into a raindrop, each of the colors, or wavelengths, of light is bent at a slightly different angle. Each of the colors is then reflected off the back of the drop, and as it bounces out of the raindrop it is again bent. In each band of the rainbow we see light reflected from the Sun at a different angle—which means it looks a different color.

HOW TO MAKE A SPECTRUM

Before you begin

You must set this experiment up on a sunny day, beside a window in direct sunlight.

You will need

- ✔ Straight-sided glass bottle filled with water
- ✔ Ruler and marker
- ✔ Reusable poster adhesive
- ✔ Black card
- ✔ Scissors

1 Mark a line down the middle of the card. Cut a slit ¼ in (0.5 cm) wide, three quarters of the way across the card.

Take it further

If you have triangular prisms of glass, you could repeat the experiment of English scientist Isaac Newton (1643–1727). He directed a beam of sunlight through a slit in the drapes into a dark room and through a triangular block of glass called a prism. When the sunbeam passed through the prism, each color of light was bent or "refracted" by the prism at a slightly different angle, and so the beam fanned out into the stunning rainbow of colors known as a spectrum. He combined the colors again by placing a second prism in the path of the light as it formed a spectrum: the colors formed white sunlight again.

3 Take the bottle of water and position it behind the slit in the black card so the sunlight shines through the glass.

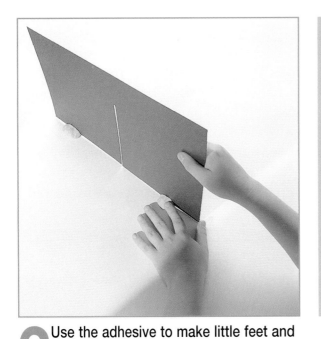

The bottle of water is splitting the white sunlight into the colors of the spectrum. These colors always appear in the same order: red, orange, yellow, green, blue, indigo, violet. To remember the order of the colors, people often use a "mnemonic," which is a sentence made up using the initial letters of the colors.

One mnemonic is Roy G Biv, but you can also make up your own with the letters ROYGBIV, such as "Running Over Yesterday's Garbage Bags Is Vile."

2 Use the adhesive to make little feet and stand the card upright. Position it on a white surface directly facing the Sun.

The light shining onto the bottle will split into several smaller beams, and a spectrum should now be visible on the paper. If it is not clear, move the bottle and card around until you can see all the colors.

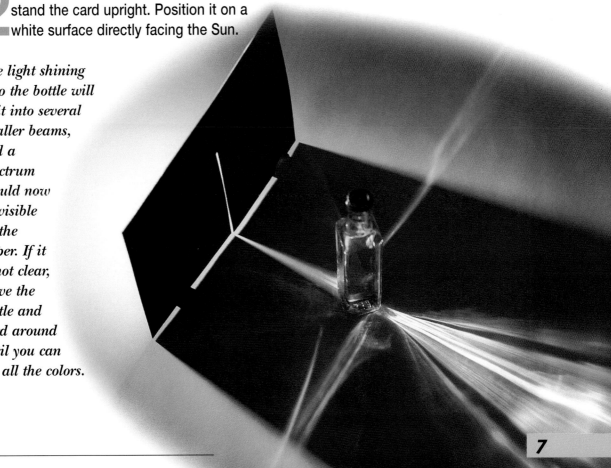

THREE-COLOR WORLD

Our eyes can only sense three different colors, red, green, and blue. This circuit board reflects a mix of these colors.

You see things in color because you have millions of special cells in your eye. There are color-sensitive cells, called cones, and light-sensitive cells, called rods. Rods can detect anything from the brightest light to the dimmest, but they cannot tell one color from another. If you only saw with rods the world would look black and white—the cones make it colorful.

Scientists think that there are three kinds of cones. Some cones are more sensitive to red

Did you know?

Carrots help you to see better in the dark because they contain vitamin A, which is known to be important in helping the rods (light-sensitive cells) in the back of our eyes to work.

THE FIRST COLOR PHOTOS

In 1806, an English scientist, Thomas Young (1773–1829), suggested that our eyes only recognize three colors of light—red, green, and blue—and every other color is a mix of these. However, this theory was hard to prove.

Half a century later, the young Scottish physicist James Clerk Maxwell (1831–1879) had an idea. He took three black-and-white photographs of a plaid ribbon—one through red glass, one through green glass, and one through blue. Each colored glass let through only light of the same color, so each picture recorded the amount of light reflecting from the ribbon in each color.

Maxwell used three projectors to display his three black-and-white photos onto a screen through three colored glasses. The picture recording the red in the plaid he projected through a red glass, so it showed red on the screen. In the same way, the picture recording the green was projected through a green glass, and the picture recording the blue was projected through a blue glass, so it showed blue on the screen. When he lined up all three pictures in the same place on the screen, the result was a full-color picture of the plaid ribbon.

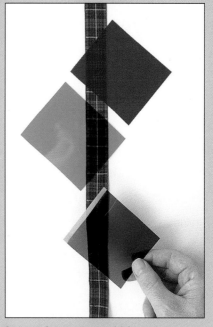

Lay red, green, and blue cellophane over a plaid ribbon, and you will see different parts of the pattern through each one. Maxwell's camera picked up different colors in the same way.

light, some are more sensitive to green, and some to blue. Amazingly, although your eyes can distinguish about ten million different colors, you are actually seeing different mixtures of these basic colors.

When the three primary colors of light (red, green, and blue) are mixed together, you get white light; if none of them is present, you get black light, or darkness. Scientists have combined two theories about

light and vision to suggest that we see colors in two stages or "zones." In the first zone, the cones in the eyes react and fire off nerve signals to the brain. In the next zone, the nerves on the way to the brain create new signals. In this zone, colors are paired together: blue with its opposite yellow, and red with green. If there is a lot of blue light, our brains turn off the yellow signals, yellow light turns off the blue signals, and so on.

HOW TO MIX COLORED LIGHT

Before you begin

Gels are sheets of translucent plastic used by photographers. They are expensive, so you may prefer to use transparent paper (cellophane).

You will need

- ✔ Red, green, and blue sheets of cellophane or gels
- ✔ Three similar flashlights
- ✔ Fine marker pen
- ✔ Adhesive tape
- ✔ A white wall
- ✔ Scissors

1 Mark and cut a circle in each of the three colored gels to fit over the end of the flashlight. Stick neatly in place.

In the real world

COLOR TV

A television picture is as full of different colors as a rainbow, but all of the colors you can see are made by mixing just three colors: red, green, and blue.

Inside your TV are electron "guns" that fire streams of electrically charged particles in beams on to the back of the TV screen. The gun fires the particles line by line, covering the whole screen in 52 millionths of a second. Where the particles hit the screen, they make it glow by heating up a special coating of dots or strips made of a chemical called phosphor, which reacts to the beam.

There are three colors of phosphor dots: red, green, and blue, arranged in groups of three (one of each color in each group). There are also three electron guns each making different colored dots glow. As the three guns sweep across the screen, and the thousands of phosphor dots glow, we see different colors, depending on how many dots of each color are glowing, and how strongly.

Because the electron guns are so fast, and because there are so many dots on the screen—over a million dots on a 24-in (60-cm) screen—we see moving images.

2 In a darkened room, shine one color on a white wall, then shine the other flashlights so you can see all three.

3 Move the circles of light around until all three are pointing at the same place. What color does the spot change to?

You should find that where all three colors overlap, the spot is white. There will be different colors in the patches where just two beams overlap.

WHAT COLOR IS IT?

Color is actually created by the light bouncing off the objects around us— whether they are plants or plastics!

Look at a red tomato, a green field, or a yellow shirt, and you might think that it is the tomato that is red, the field that is green, and the shirt that is yellow. If so, you would be wrong. It is not the tomato that is red, but the light you see it by. Only sources of light such as the Sun, or a flashlight, have their own colors. Everything else "borrows" its color from the light you see it by.

Things borrow their color by reflecting some of the light shining on them, and soaking up the rest. Whenever light falls on a surface, the surface soaks

Did you know?

In hot climates, people often paint their houses white. The white paint reflects all the colors in the sunlight, so the walls do not absorb any light and therefore do not warm up.

up some colors of light, and they are turned into heat. The other colors bounce back, and these are the colors you see.

Sunshine contains all the colors of the rainbow. The skin of a tomato absorbs (soaks up) every color but red. So when you see a flower looking yellow in the sunshine, you are seeing just the yellow rays of sunshine, which the flower reflects, and not all the other colors, which it absorbs.

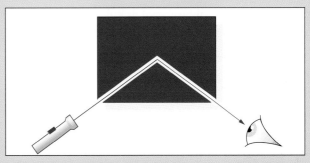

In focus

SEEING DIFFERENT COLORS

Different things are different colors because the tiny atoms and molecules in their surfaces are different. Some atoms and molecules are very self-contained and bounce back nearly all the light that hits them, making them pale whitish colors because all the colors are mixed together and diluted.

Other colors occur because the molecules that they are made of are very ready to absorb a great deal of the colors in the light shining on them, so the color left to bounce back at you is pure and strong. The molecules of dyes, for instance, have complex structures, which are so good at soaking up colors of light that the color they bounce back is intense.

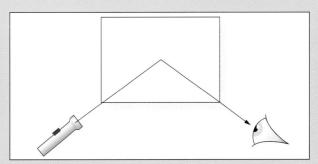

If you bounce light off a surface that looks white, all the colors are reflected: you see white light.

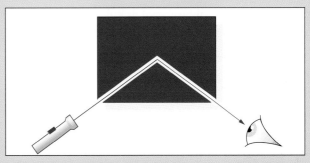

If you bounce light off something that looks red, all the colors of the spectrum apart from red are absorbed: only red light reaches your eye.

MAKING OBJECTS CHANGE COLOR

You will need

✔ A cardboard shoe box, painted white inside

✔ Red, yellow, and green vegetables

✔ Sheets of red and green cellophane

✔ A flashlight or desk lamp

✔ Scissors

✔ Tape

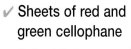

1 Cut a large hole in the lid of the shoe box, and a smaller hole in one end. Cut a sheet of green cellophane to fit the lid.

What is happening?

Everything but a light source gets its color from the light falling on it. For example, a lemon looks yellow only because it reflects yellow from the light falling on it. If there is no yellow in the light falling on the lemon, it will look black, no matter how bright the light, because the lemon reflects no other colors but yellow.

In the same way, a sheet of white paper will look the same color as the light that is falling on it because if it is white, it must reflect all colors equally. In red light, white paper will look red. In yellow light it will look yellow, and so on.

4 Now remove the green cellophane and replace it with the red. Put the lid back on the box and check the colors again.

2 Put the colored vegetables in the box. Tape the cellophane over the hole in the lid and replace the lid on the box.

3 Turn off the lights. Shine the desk lamp or flashlight into the hole in the end of the box, and look at the vegetables.

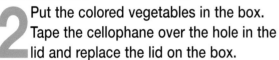

With the green cellophane in place (step 3, above) the green vegetable is dark green, the red vegetable is rich brown, and the yellow vegetable is pale green. However, under the red cellophane the green vegetable becomes brown, the yellow vegetable is orange, and the red vegetable is dark red.

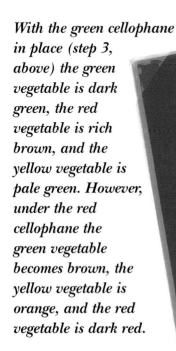

MIXING COLORS

When we mix colored paints, we can create almost any color we want; but which colors should we mix to create the color we want? On page 9, red, green, and blue were said to be the three primary colors. This may have surprised you, if you have been told by your parents or art teacher that the three primary colors are red, yellow, and blue.

If you want to create good color paintings, you must start with the primary colors.

Did you know?

Red, green, and blue light are sometimes called the additive primaries, because you can make any other color by adding them together in different amounts. Yellow, magenta, and cyan are sometimes called the subtractive primaries, because they absorb colors from white light, leaving only the color that you can see.

However, this is not the contradiction it seems.

Red, green, and blue are indeed the primary colors of light. They are the three colors our eyes are sensitive to. Red, green, and blue light can be mixed in different proportions to make any color under the Sun. And mixed together in equal proportions, red, green, and blue light make white light.

But red, yellow, and blue—or colors similar to them—are the primary colors of paints, dyes, inks, and all surfaces that are not light sources. The red and the blue are not the same as the red and blue of the primary colors of light, but colors that are a mix of the two. The red is a purply red called magenta. The blue is a greeny blue called cyan. The primary colors of paints, inks, and dyes are magenta, yellow, and cyan.

Add all three primary colors of light together and you get the sum of all colors of light—white. But magenta, yellow, and cyan paints work in the opposite way. None of these paints has any color of its own. The only color each has is from the light that shines on it, so the color you see is white light minus any color the paints absorb. Just as the three primary colors of light can be mixed to give every other color, so primary pigments can be mixed to give almost any color you want.

In focus

PRINTING COLORS

All the colors in this book were made by using magenta, yellow, and cyan inks (plus black). Each color picture is "separated" through magenta, yellow, and cyan filters to give three different films, one in each color. These films (or pictures) are called color separations. The printers use them to make three printing plates. The three separations are printed on top of each other in exactly the same place on the page. The three inks mix to give the full range of colors.

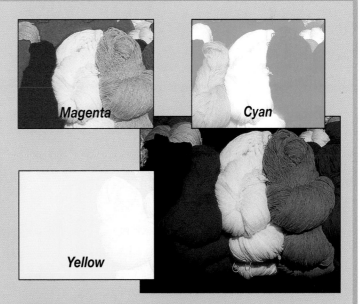

When the three different separations (the cyan, magenta, and yellow shown above) are printed on top of each other, the result is a perfect full-color picture.

HOW TO CREATE A COLOR WHEEL

Before you begin

REMEMBER:

✔ A magenta paint soaks up green light and reflects a mix of red and blue.

✔ A yellow paint soaks up blue light and reflects a mix of green and red.

✔ A cyan paint soaks up red light and reflects a mix of green and blue.

You will need

✔ Yellow, magenta, and cyan paints

✔ A plate to draw around

✔ A fine marker pen

✔ A paint palette

✔ A paintbrush

✔ White paper

✔ A ruler

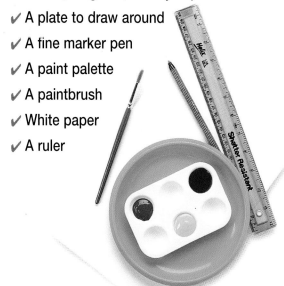

What is happening?

Mixing two primary colors of paint together absorbs two-thirds of the spectrum, leaving only one to reflect: magenta and yellow soak up green and blue light, leaving only red; yellow and cyan soaks up blue and red light, leaving only green; cyan and magenta soaks up red and green, leaving only blue.

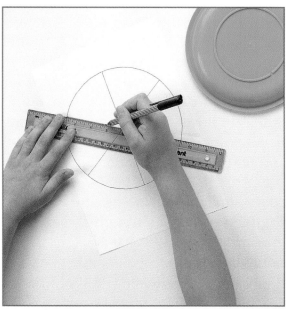

1 Use the plate to draw a circle on the paper. Mark the center, then divide the circle into six rougly equal segments.

3 Now mix equal quantities of yellow and magenta to get red. Paint the red in between the yellow and magenta.

Take it further

Mixing all three primary colors of paint together absorbs three-thirds of the spectrum, leaving nothing but darkness (although unless you have very pure colors you will get a dirty brown shade). Red, green, and blue light are each a third of the full spectrum of colors, so they add up to make the full spectrum of white light.

Mix the cyan and magenta. You will get deep blue paint, with which to complete the color wheel. Use it as a guide when you are mixing paints.

2 Paint one segment yellow, one magenta, and one cyan. Leave blank segments between each of the colors.

4 Now mix a little yellow and cyan. You will get green. Use this to fill in between the yellow and cyan.

COLOR CHANGES

Did you know?

Ordinary photography takes pictures of visible light, but photographs can also capture images using infrared. This is the part of the electromagnetic spectrum that lies just beyond red light. Infrared film can see through dust and pollution in the atmosphere, so it is very useful for taking pictures of large areas of earth from the air. These pictures can reveal areas of damaged vegetation that might not be clear from the ground.

Bright sunlight is said to be white light because it is a mix of nearly every color of light. But it is not actually pure white, because some colors are there in higher proportions than others and some colors are missing altogether. When young children paint the Sun yellow in pictures, they are not so far wrong—even though if you could look at the Sun safely you would see it looks almost white. Sunshine is slightly yellow because it reaches us through the atmosphere, which acts as a filter. Our eyes are adjusted to this slight yellowness so that we usually see it as white. As the Sun sinks towards the horizon in evening, it can turn more yellow, orange, or even red as the atmosphere cuts out more and more of its blue light.

Every source of whitish light has some colors missing or boosted. Our eyes are quick to adjust to these slight differences so that we do not always notice them. Ordinary electric light contains extra orange light. Candlelight is more orangey still. Fluorescent light actually contains an excess of green.

At rock concerts and on the stage, directors often use lighting to create special effects. By shining colored lights on colored clothes or backdrops our eyes become confused, but the effect is exciting.

Take it further

HEALTHY COLORS
Because most things we see get their color by reflecting some of the light that falls on them, they can look different in different kinds of light. You might have already noticed how people often look far healthier and fitter, for instance, in the warm yellowish glow of a golden sunset than they do under a gray overcast sky. Some food stores have recognized this fact and make use of it to make food look riper or more enticing with specially designed fluorescent lights that boost or cut out certain colors. You can see how they do this for yourself by trying out this simple experiment.

• Use a desk lamp with a low wattage bulb, and cut sheets of colored cellophane to hold over the lamp. (Do not hold the cellophane too near the light bulb, as even low wattage bulbs can give out enough heat to melt the cellophane.)

• Arrange a bowl of fruit or colored objects on the table top beneath the lamp. Try several different colors, and look to see which makes the fruit look more attractive.

This fruit has been photographed under white light.

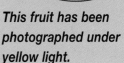

This fruit has been photographed under yellow light.

This fruit has been photographed under blue light.

COLOR BLINDNESS

Nobody has any real idea whether people see colors in the same way. Most people see the same range of colors. However, there are some people who cannot distinguish between all the colors that most other people can. These people are said to be color blind. Usually, color blindness results from a

Did you know?

Most mammals, apart from humans and other primates, are color blind. However, fish, reptiles, and some amphibians and birds do see the full spectrum of color. In the insect world, butterflies and bees depend on color vision for recognizing the flowers that provide nectar.

TEST YOURSELF FOR COLOR BLINDNESS

Blindness to red is called protanopia; to green is duteranopia; and to blue is tritanopia. Someone who is red-blind cannot tell the difference between red and green, while someone who is green-blind cannot tell green from orange-browns, and someone who is blue-blind cannot tell blue from yellow.

This is one of the color blindness tests used by opticians. Look at the spotty circle and decide which number(s) you can see. If you have normal vision, you can see the number 42 in tones of red on a gray background. If you have blindness to red, you can see the number 2; if you have blindness to green you can only see the number 4.

Colors mean different things to different people. If you are color blind, it does not mean that you see only black and white, but that you cannot distinguish between certain colors, so, for example, red and green may look the same.

defect in one or more of the three kinds of cones (cells in our eyes that are sensitive to red, green, and blue), and so color-blind people cannot see one, two, or all of these colors.

Red/green color blindness is by far the most common form. But while one in 12 boys suffer from it, only one in 200 girls do. This is because this kind of color blindness is a defect that is inherited or "genetic."

We have two genes for every characteristic we inherit, and people who are red/green color blind have a defective red cone gene. The red cone gene is a "recessive gene," which means that you are only color blind if

there is no alternative gene. Genetic information is carried on chromosomes, which are inside the cells in our bodies.

There are two sex chromosomes, X and Y. The red cone gene is carried on the X. Girls have two X chromosomes, so even if a girl does inherit the color blindness gene on one of her X chromosomes, the chances are she will have the healthy red cone gene on the other X. This will override the faulty gene and give her normal color vision. A boy, however, has only one X chromosome (and only one Y), so a faulty gene on the X chromosome will make him color blind.

LOOKING AT COLOR CONTRASTS

You will need

- ✔ White paper cut into small squares
- ✔ Paints in bright colors
- ✔ A paintbrush

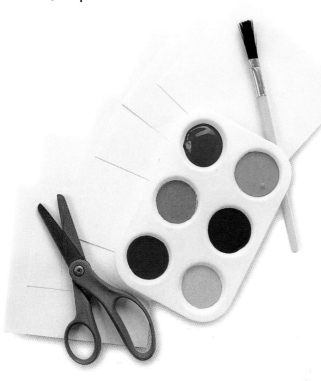

1 Paint a color on each sheet of paper and lay them out, widely spaced. List the colors in the order of brightness.

What is happening?

You might think that how bright or dim a color looks depends entirely on how much light it reflects. This is true if there are no other colors around. But as soon as other colors come into play our eyes start playing tricks. The brightness of colors more often than not depends on just what the neighboring colors are. Next to one color a red might zing with brightness; next to another it might look quite dull.

2 Pick out pairs of colors: try laying an orange patch next to a green patch. Look at the contrast and brightness.

In the real world

GREEN SKIN

Neighboring colors not only affect brightness; they can also change the color you see. Many painters have noticed this and made use of it in their paintings. When painting a white horse in a green field, for instance, they include a little pink paint in the white used for the horse so it does not look sickly. Shadows are blacker versions of the same color, or may even be complementary colors: for example, shadows on sand are purplish. This is why the French painter Pierre-Auguste Renoir (1841–1919) often used bright green as shadows on pink skin—and it looked perfectly natural.

Green shadows enhance the flesh tones of the girls in this detail of a painting by Renoir.

3 Then try laying a yellow patch next to a purple patch. Does your judgement of brightness change at all?

Compare different color combinations and see how the color contrast affects their brightness.

COLOR WAVES

All color comes from the tiny electrons that zoom around the nucleus (center) of an atom. When an atom is heated in the Sun or energized by an electric spark, it gets "excited" and one of its electrons may be pushed further out. It is said to be pushed to a higher energy level; this is a bit like stretching an elastic band.

Then, as if the band were released, the electron slips back in again and, as it does, it fires off a "photon," a little package of light. The wavelength or color of the photon fired off depends on the size of the

Did you know?

Sodium street lamps glow deep yellow because yellow is the emission color for sodium, while neon lights are typically red because neon's emission color is red. The red glow of a sodium street lamp just after it is switched on is due to the presence of neon. The sodium is solid at normal temperatures, so the red neon light heats up the sodium until it is warm enough to vaporize, giving its intense yellow light and swamping the red neon.

Sodium and neon lights, seen in Miami, Florida, are both decorative and practical.

electron's jump as it pings back to its normal level. This, in turn, depends on the structure of the atom. This is why when any gas glows, it sends out its own unique range of colors, called its emission spectrum. Hydrogen, sodium, neon, and every other element each has its own distinctive color.

Atoms can only send out certain colors, and they can only absorb certain colors. This is called an absorption pattern.

In focus

EXCITED ATOMS

Exciting an atom into firing off photons of light requires energy. Usually this energy comes from electrons and other atoms bashing into it. In electric lights, the thin wire of the filament means that whizzing electrons are crowded together and collide with atom after atom, prodding them into sending out billions of photons. Atoms stimulated in this way send out light of all kinds of different wavelengths in an incoherent jumble. Light from light bulbs, the Sun, and virtually every other source of light similarly sends out a collection of different wavelengths of light. This is why light from these sources is white, which is basically no color in particular.

However if the atoms are only stimulated by photons of light and photons of a particular wavelength, they will send out all the light at certain wavelengths, and all the waves will be in perfect step. The only time this ever happens is in a laser. This is what makes laser beams so special. Uniquely,

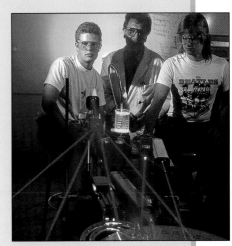

A laser sends out a concentrated beam of light.

there is only one wavelength and so only one color of light in a laser beam. All the waves are "coherent," which means that they all travel absolutely together. A beam of red light on a stage set may look like a red laser beam, but it usually contains a mix of many different red wavelengths. A laser beam is just one wavelength, so it is very concentrated—and has a lot of power for very little energy.

SEEING SHIMMERING COLORS

You will need

- ✔ Ordinary dishwashing liquid
- ✔ 2–3 tablespoons of sugar
- ✔ An empty bottle
- ✔ A large bowl
- ✔ Wire

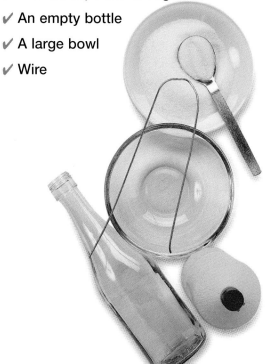

1 Stir the dishwashing liquid into an equal amount of water and add the sugar to make a really thick solution.

What is happening?

These shimmering (or iridescent) colors come from the way the surfaces bend rays of sunlight, splitting sunlight into its separate colors. Sometimes the effect is like a rainbow. The sunbeam is simply split into its component colors, and the color you see depends on the combination of the angle at which the Sun strikes the surface and the angle you see it from. The color changes as the surface shifts in the breeze or as you alter your viewpoint slightly.

3 Dip the loop into the soap solution and draw it out slowly so that the film of soap is held across the hoop.

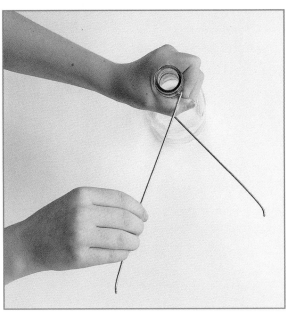

2 Wrap the wire around the neck of the bottle, forming a loop about 1 in (2.5 cm) across. Twist the ends together.

IRIDESCENT COLORS

Birds such as peacocks and hummingbirds, mallards and pheasants, and insects such as dragonflies, bluebottles, and beetles all have shimmering, iridescent colors. What makes them iridescent is minute ridges in a transparent layer on the surface of their feathers, wings, or bodies.

A spider's web hung with dew, and iridescent feathers or wings, can look colorless and dull when clouds are over the Sun. Then suddenly, as the Sun comes out, they flash in brilliant colors that shimmer with the slightest movement. You can see the same shimmering colors in bubbles, on CDs, and on oil patches on wet roads.

Can you see colors in the loop? Blow through the loop and you will be able to make a stream of iridescent bubbles.

Experiments in Science

Science is about knowledge: it is concerned with knowing and trying to understand the world around us. The word comes from the Latin word, *scire*, to know.

In the early 17th century, the great English thinker Francis Bacon suggested that the best way to learn about the world was not simply to think about it, but to go out and look for yourself—to make observations and try things out. Ever since then, scientists have tried to approach their work with a mixture of observation and experiment. Scientists insist that an idea or theory must be tested by observation and experiment before it is widely accepted.

All the experiments in this book have been tried before, and the theories behind them are widely accepted. But that is no reason why you should accept them. Once you have done all the experiments in this book, you will know that the ideas are true not because we have told you that they are but because you have seen for yourself.

All too often in science there is an external factor interfering with the result which the scientist just has not thought of. Sometimes this can make the experiment seem to work when it has not, as well as making it fail. One scientist conducted lots of demonstrations to show that a clever horse called Hans could count things and tap out the answer with his hoof. The horse was indeed clever, but later it was found that rather than counting, he was getting clues from tiny unconscious movements of the scientist's eyebrows.

This is why it is very important when conducting experiments to be as rigorous as you possibly can. The more casual you are, the more "eyebrow factors" you will let in. There will always be some things that you cannot control. But the more precise you are, the less these are likely to affect the outcome.

What went wrong?

However careful you are, your experiments may not work. If so, you should try to find out where you went wrong. Then repeat the experiment until you are absolutely sure you are doing everything right. Scientists learn as much, if not more, from experiments that go wrong as those that succeed. In 1929, Alexander Fleming discovered the first antibiotic drug, penicillin, when he noticed that a bacteria culture he was growing for an experiment had gone moldy—and that the mold seemed to kill the bacteria. A poor scientist would probably have thrown the moldy culture away. A good scientist is one who looks for alternative explanations for unexpected results.

Glossary

Absorption: The opposite of radiation—the soaking up of light, heat, sound, and other forms of energy. When light strikes a surface, the surface absorbs some light and reflects the rest.

Additive primary colors: These are the three basic colors of light—red, green, and blue—which can be added together in different proportions to make every other color in the rainbow. Adding all three together at full strength makes white.

Atoms: Every substance is made of invisibly tiny atoms, which are the smallest particle of any chemical element. Each atom has a nucleus, around which minute electrons whirl.

Chromosome: A coil of DNA that contains lots of different genes.

Coherent: Light is coherent if the waves that make it up are all traveling "in step" with each other.

Electron: A tiny particle that whizzes around the nucleus of an atom. When atoms absorb light, electrons gain energy. When atoms radiate light, electrons lose energy.

Fluorescent light: A light that works by a gas in a tube being excited as an electric current is passed through it. The gas then gives out photons, either directly as in neon lamps, or indirectly by hitting a coating of phosphor on the outside of the tube, which then glows.

Gene: A string of molecules of the chemical DNA. It contains the information that passes from parent to child and determines how the child will grow.

Laser: A device that produces a very powerful, coherent beam of light of just one color. The word laser stands for "Light Amplification by Stimulated Emission of Radiation."

Photons: Tiny packets of light and other kinds of electromagnetic radiation, so small they have almost no weight at all. They may be either waves or particles.

Primary colors: *See* Additive primary colors and Subtractive primary colors.

Radiation: The movement of photons and other subatomic particles (particles within an atom).

Subtractive primary colors: The three basic colors of pigments and paints— yellow, cyan, and magenta— which can be mixed together to make every other color in the rainbow. They are called subtractive because they absorb (subtract) all other colors from white light. Mixing all three colors together full strength makes black.

Translucent: Something is translucent if light can shine through it, so a pane of glass is translucent.

Index